Healing Earth, Healing Ourselves

Simple Steps to Sustainable Living and Personal Wellness

Iris R Bell, MD PhD

Creative Bookworm Press

Copyright © 2024 by Dr. Iris R Bell and Creative Bookworm LLC

All rights reserved.

No portion of this book may be reproduced in any form without written permission from the publisher or author, except as permitted by U.S. copyright law.

HEALTH & MEDICAL DISCLAIMER

Books by Dr. Bell

Getting Whole, Getting Well: Healing Holistically from Chronic Illness

Inflammation 101: Natural Solutions Beyond the Anti Inflammatory Diet

Chew on Things – It Helps You Think: Words of Wisdom from a Worried Canine

Chew on Things: Workbook for Fellow Worriers

Healing Earth, Healing Ourselves: Simple Steps to Sustainable Living and Personal Wellness

Natural Brain Boosters: Improve Memory, Focus, and Mental Clarity for Seniors

Claim Your FREE GIFT

D ear Reader -

Thanks for reading my book!

As a thank you, I'd like to offer you a FREE guide on our Toxin-Free Living Blueprint. It is a concise shorter summary of things to consider in your journey toward a healthier environment for you, your family, and our planet. You'll also receive a FREE Sustainable Supplies Checklist to support you in further exploring this important topic.

Just click below to claim your free guide and future email updates about future books and relevant news related to this book.

See you soon...

Visit us at:

https://www.dynamicselfcare.com/toxin-free-living-blueprint-offer

Contents

Preface

Your personal environment profoundly impacts your health, well-being, and quality of life.

The air you breathe, the water you drink, and the products you use can either nourish or harm your body.

In today's modern world, you're exposed to a staggering array of toxins, contaminants, and pollutants on a daily basis.

These environmental toxins can accumulate in your body over time, leading to chronic health issues and accelerated aging.

A cutting-edge study by the Environmental Working Group found that the average newborn baby has 287 known toxins in their umbilical cord blood.

This means that even before taking their first breath, babies are already burdened with a toxic load that can impact their health for years to come.

As you age, this toxic burden only increases, as you're exposed to more and more pollutants in your environment.

From the BPA in plastic containers to the phthalates in personal care products, these chemicals can disrupt your hormones, damage your cells, and contribute to a wide range of health problems.

But here's the good news: you have the power to take control of your personal environment and reduce your toxic exposure.

By making simple, conscious choices about the products you use and the way you live, you can create a cleaner, greener, and healthier environment for yourself and your loved ones.

This book will show you how to detoxify your home, your body, and your life, using natural, holistic approaches that are backed by science.

You'll learn about the hidden toxins in your environment, and how to eliminate them from your life.

You'll find out about powerful detoxification techniques that can help your body eliminate stored toxins and restore balance.

And you'll find practical, actionable tips for creating a healthier, more sustainable lifestyle that supports your long-term health and well-being.

Chapter 1: Understanding Environmental Issues and Their Impact on Health

Emma had always considered herself healthy. She ate well, exercised regularly, and visited her doctor for annual check-ups.

However, one day she found herself struggling to breathe during a routine jog.

A visit to urgent care revealed that Emma had developed asthma - an alarming diagnosis for someone with no previous history of respiratory issues.

The culprit? The worsening air quality in her city due to increasing pollution levels.

Emma's story serves as a stark reminder of how environmental issues can directly impact personal health.

Understanding these environmental challenges and their implications is the first step towards safeguarding your health. This chapter aims to shed light on key environmental issues such as climate change, pollution, resource depletion and explain their connections to human health.

"Climate Change: A Public Health Emergency"

Climate change is arguably the most significant environmental issue we face today. Rising global temperatures due to greenhouse gas emissions have far-reaching effects on our planet's ecosystems and subsequently on human health.

According to a report by a leading medical journal, *The Lancet*, "climate change could be the greatest global health threat of the 21st century." It increases heat-related illnesses during extremely hot weather and exacerbates respiratory problems due to poor air quality caused by wildfire smoke or pollens. What mainstream medicine usually overlooks is the danger of additional damaging exposures such as toxic pesticides and herbicides people use in their homes to get rid of bugs and weeds. And lately, there is increased risk from molds and mold toxins in flood-damaged homes.

"Air Quality: Breathe Easier"

Air pollution from vehicle emissions, industrial processes, and even indoor sources like cooking fumes or synthetic materials can lead to severe respiratory conditions like asthma, allergies, or lung cancer.

As Emma learned firsthand, reducing exposure to air pollutants is crucial for maintaining good respiratory health. Start by monitoring local air quality indexes and limit outdoor activities during periods of high pollution.

"Water Contamination: Quenching Thirst Safely"

Clean water is essential for life - however, water sources worldwide are increasingly contaminated with harmful substances such as heavy metals, pesticides, and microplastics. These contaminants can cause chronic illnesses including kidney damage or hormonal disruptions.

Ensuring you drink and cook with clean, filtered water is a practical step towards reducing your exposure to these harmful substances. Heat foods in oven- or microwave-safe glass and stainless steel pots and pans rather than in plastic trays and containers.

"Reducing Chemical Exposure: A Less Toxic Life"

From household cleaners to personal care products, we're surrounded by synthetic chemicals. While some are harmless, others can interfere with our hormonal systems and immune function.

Opt for natural alternatives whenever possible. For instance, vinegar and baking soda can replace many conventional cleaning products.

Choose personal care items free of parabens and phthalates to reduce your chemical load further.

The Bottom Line: Protecting Health through Environmental Stewardship

Environmental health is deeply intertwined with personal health. Ignoring the environmental issues that surround us can put our well-being at risk, just as it did for Emma.

By understanding these challenges and taking steps such as monitoring air quality, ensuring clean drinking water, reducing plastic use, avoiding synthetic chemicals, and supporting cleaner energy solutions - can we safeguard our health and contribute to a healthier planet. Many manufacturers bow to consumer demands and choices – witness the growth of availability of organic-grown foods in your local supermarket in recent years.

Your actions count. Start small, but start now.

As Margaret Mead famously said, *"Never doubt that a small group of thoughtful committed citizens can change the world - indeed, it's the only thing that ever has."*

Now, let's dig deeper into some specifics of how the environment can affect your personal health, the health of your family. The environment is not some abstract idea that politicians argue about - the environment should matter to you for very core reasons of living a healthier, happier life.

The Health Impact of Environmental Toxins: How Cleaning Up Your Environment Protects Your Health

What Are Environmental Toxins?

We hear the word "toxins" a lot these days, but what are they really? Toxins are harmful substances that can be found in the air we breathe, the water we drink, the food we eat, and even the products we use at home. Some of these toxins are natural, but many come from chemicals made by people. They can sneak into our bodies and cause health problems over time.

Many health issues we deal with today—like asthma, heart disease, cancer, and even autism and learning problems—can be linked to these environmental toxins. The good news? By making small changes in our lives, we can protect ourselves and our families from these harmful chemicals. Let's take a closer look at how toxins affect our health and what we can do to stay safe.

Toxins and Autism: What's the Link?

Autism Spectrum Disorder (ASD) is a condition that affects how a person communicates, behaves, and interacts with others. Scientists don't fully understand what causes autism, but they believe it comes from both genetics and the environment. This means that exposure to certain chemicals during pregnancy or in early childhood may increase the chances of developing autism.

Some studies have found that air pollution and pesticides are linked to a higher risk of autism. For example, children born to mothers who were exposed to high levels of air pollution during pregnancy have a greater chance of being diagnosed with autism. Another study found that women who lived near farms that used a lot of pesticides had a higher likelihood of having children with autism.

What Can You Do?

- Choose organic fruits and vegetables whenever you can to reduce exposure to pesticides.

- Improve the air quality in your home by using air purifiers and keeping windows open for ventilation.

- Avoid areas with heavy traffic and air pollution, especially during pregnancy.

Heart Disease and the Air We Breathe

Did you know that the air you breathe can affect your heart? Air pollution isn't just bad for your lungs—it can also damage your heart and blood vessels. When we breathe in dirty air, tiny particles can enter our bloodstream and cause inflammation, which is one of the leading causes of heart disease.

Studies show that people who live in areas with a lot of air pollution are more likely to have heart attacks and strokes. But it's not just air pollution that's dangerous—chemicals like BPA, found in some plastics, have also been linked to heart problems. BPA can mess with hormones in your body, leading to health issues like heart disease and diabetes.

What Can You Do?

- Try to limit your time outdoors on days when the air

quality is bad.

- Use air purifiers inside your home to reduce indoor air pollution. Look for purifiers with good activated carbon and HEPA filter components. Newer models are also quiet for use while sleeping.

- Choose BPA-free plastic containers, or better yet, switch to glass or stainless steel for storing food and drinks.

Cancer and the Chemicals Around Us

When it comes to cancer, there are many things that can increase our risk—genetics, lifestyle choices, and yes, environmental toxins. Some chemicals in our environment can damage the cells in our bodies, leading to cancer over time. These chemicals include things like pesticides, air pollutants, and even certain ingredients in everyday products.

One common chemical linked to cancer is glyphosate, which is found in many weed killers. Studies have shown that people who use products with glyphosate regularly have a higher risk of getting certain types of cancer, like non-Hodgkin lymphoma.

Chemicals found in plastics, like BPA, have also been linked to breast cancer, prostate cancer, and other cancers. These chemicals can disrupt our hormones, which play a big role in how our cells grow and function.

What Can You Do?

- Use natural weed killers in your garden or try non-chemical methods like mulching to keep weeds at bay.

- Avoid heating food in plastic containers, as the heat can cause chemicals to leach into your food. Stick with glass or stainless steel.

- Buy organic foods when possible to limit your exposure to pesticides.

Autoimmune Diseases and Environmental Triggers

Autoimmune diseases happen when your body's immune system, which normally fights off infections, starts attacking your own tissues. Some common autoimmune diseases include lupus, rheumatoid arthritis, and multiple sclerosis. But did you know that environmental toxins might trigger these diseases?

Chemicals like mercury, lead, and pesticides can confuse the immune system, making it attack healthy cells. For example, people who are exposed to high levels of mercury—often from contaminated water or seafood—are more likely to develop autoimmune diseases.

Another condition called Multiple Chemical Sensitivity (MCS) is linked to exposure to everyday chemicals. People with MCS get sick not just when they are around pesticides and herbicides, but also when they're around things like natural gas stoves and heat, cleaning products, perfumes, paint, car exhaust, or even air "fresheners". Over time, repeated exposure to these chemicals may lead to more serious health problems, including autoimmune diseases.

Recent research has also linked the mechanisms of MCS with a condition known as mast cell activation syndrome (MCAS). MCAS is a condition where mast cells, a type of immune cell that is naturally distributed throughout the body in loose connective tissue surfaces (e.g., the skin), release too many inflammatory substances like histamine. This can lead to symptoms such as allergic reactions, digestive problems, and fatigue. Chronic inflammation is bad for anyone's health – finding ways to stop causing inflammation is essential.

For MCAS, a histamine avoidance diet—which limits foods like aged cheeses and other fermented items that are either high in histamine or trigger mast cell activation—can help reduce symptoms. Additionally, taking diamine oxidase (DAO) enzyme supplements may help break down excess histamine from food, offering relief. Natural supplements like quercetin and luteolin may help stabilize mast cells, preventing them from releasing histamine and other inflammatory substances, potentially offering further support for managing MCAS. A subset of doctors specialize in managing MCAS, and you may want to consult an expert on this condition for individual guidance and treatment

What Can You Do?

- Use natural cleaning products that don't contain harsh chemicals. Look for fragrance-free options to avoid artificial scents.

- Filter your tap water to reduce heavy metals like lead and mercury.

- Choose personal care products without synthetic fragrances or chemicals known to trigger allergic reactions.

How Toxins Affect Your Brain

Our brains are delicate, and toxins in the environment can have a big impact on how they function. Diseases like Alzheimer's, Parkinson's, and other neurodegenerative conditions have been linked to exposure to harmful chemicals.

Pesticides, in particular, have been linked to Parkinson's disease. Farmers and people who work with pesticides have been shown to have a higher risk of developing this illness. These chemicals can damage brain cells and cause them to die over time.

Heavy metals like lead and aluminum are also dangerous for brain health. Long-term exposure to lead, for example, can cause memory problems, learning difficulties, and perhaps even increase the risk of Alzheimer's disease. In addition, recent studies also link higher levels of air pollution, especially from long-term exposures or even from wildfires, to the development of dementia (https://pubmed.ncbi.nlm.nih.gov/37578757/).

What Can You Do?

- Choose organic produce to limit your exposure to pesticides.

- Use water filters to remove heavy metals like lead from your drinking water.as well as other chemical contaminants

- Avoid aluminum-containing products, such as certain deodorants and cookware.

Allergies and Breathing Problems Caused by Toxins

If you or your family members have allergies or asthma, environmental toxins could be making things worse. Air pollution, mold, and chemicals in cleaning products can trigger asthma attacks and cause allergic reactions. Even the air inside your home can be full of harmful chemicals from things like paint, furniture, and household cleaners.

Children, in particular, are more sensitive to these toxins. Studies show that kids who live in areas with high levels of air pollution are more likely to develop asthma. Mold in the home can also cause breathing problems and make allergies worse.

What Can You Do?

- Keep the air in your home clean by using air purifiers and opening windows for fresh air.

- Clean with natural, unscented, non-toxic products to avoid harsh chemicals.

- Fix any leaks in your home to prevent mold from growing in damp areas. If you do find mold in your home, seek help from professionals who use less toxic ways to clean it up, e.g., using natural mold killing materials like thyme oil rather than more toxic fungicides.

Living a Toxin-Free Life for Better Health

Now that you know how harmful toxins can be to your health, the next step is taking action to reduce your exposure. The good news is that small changes can make a big difference! By choosing natural products, eating organic foods, and keeping your air and water clean, you can protect yourself and your family from the dangers of environmental toxins.

Taking steps to live a more toxin-free life not only helps you feel better physically, but it can also give you peace of mind knowing that you're doing your part to create a safer, healthier world for everyone.

Chapter 2:
Sustainable Eating:
A Win-Win for Your
Health and the
Planet

Picture this. Every day, Sarah would stop by her favorite fast food joint on her way home from work, ordering a cheeseburger with a side of fries.

Her taste buds were satisfied, but she began noticing changes in her body and mood.

Along with an increase in weight, she felt sluggish and lacked energy.

One day, while waiting in line at the fast food restaurant, she overheard a conversation about sustainable eating. Intrigued, Sarah decided to do some research when she got home that night.

Armed with newfound knowledge about the positive impact of sustainable eating on personal health and the environment, Sarah made a decision to change her habits. She gradually transitioned to a more plant-based diet and started supporting local farmers by purchasing organic produce at farmer's markets.

Over time, Sarah felt more energetic and noticed improvements in her overall health. The cherry on top?

She was contributing to preserving the environment too!

Just like Sarah's transformational journey, this chapter is dedicated to helping you understand how your dietary choices can significantly influence both your health and the planet we all call home.

Understanding Plant-Based Diets

Transitioning toward a plant-based diet is one of the most effective ways to reduce your carbon footprint. This doesn't necessarily mean you have to become vegetarian or vegan overnight - even small changes can make a big difference.

The University of Oxford found that "shifting towards diets that are rich in plants could reduce greenhouse gas emissions by up to 73%."

Incorporating more fruits, vegetables, whole grains, legumes into your meals reduces environmental impact and provides essential nutrients for optimal health.

Embracing Organic Foods

Organic farming practices minimize soil degradation and water pollution while promoting biodiversity – all crucial for maintaining ecological balance.

Choosing organic products also means reducing exposure to harmful pesticides often found in conventionally grown produce. The Environmental Working Group reports that "people who eat organic produce have lower levels of pesticide residues in their bodies."

Shopping Local: A Sustainable Choice

Purchasing locally sourced food reduces the carbon footprint associated with long-distance transportation of goods. Besides, local foods often taste better and retain more nutrients because they are fresher.

Reducing Food Waste

Food waste is an often overlooked aspect of sustainable eating. By planning your meals, storing food correctly, and composting scraps, you can significantly reduce waste while contributing to a healthier environment.

The Bottom Line: Embrace Sustainable Eating for Health and Environmental Benefits

Adopting sustainable eating habits is about making choices that are beneficial for both your health and the planet. The journey may start with small steps like Sarah's - incorporating more plant-based foods into your meals or choosing organic produce when possible.

Remember, every effort counts! Just as Sarah experienced a transformation in her health and well-being through her new dietary choices, so can you.

With understanding and commitment to sustainable eating, you are paving the way to better personal health and a healthier planet for generations to come.

From an industry expert: "Sustainable food choices like plant-based diets can significantly reduce environmental impact and improve health" - Dr Marco Springmann at Oxford University's Future of Food programme

Chapter 3: Minimalism: Your Pathway to a Healthier You and Planet

It was on an average Tuesday when Susan finally snapped. She looked around her house, at the piles of clothes that never seemed to diminish, at the drawers bursting with knick-knacks she didn't remember buying, at the stacks of unread books gathering dust.

Her home, once a refuge from the world's chaos, had become a source of stress.

She was constantly cleaning, organizing, and yet it never felt like enough. The clutter wasn't just in her home - it had seeped into her mental space too.

She was always tired, perpetually distracted, and seldom content.

That's when Susan decided to take control and began the process towards minimalism.

Much like Susan's experience, many people are beginning to recognize that more isn't necessarily better. In fact, less can be liberating - for both you and our planet.

This chapter will guide you through understanding the philosophy of minimalism and how reducing your material consumption can lead to improved well-being and a healthier environment.

Understanding Minimalism as a Lifestyle Choice

Minimalism is about focusing on what truly matters in life by eliminating excess. It's not about owning specific numbers of items or living in extreme austerity - instead, this involves reducing distractions so you can focus on what brings you joy and purpose. And this approach may be better for your personal health, not just the environment.

Investing in fewer but better quality items means less waste going into landfills - a win for our planet. As Duane Elgin once said "we are moving from mindless overconsumption to conscious understatement."

Adopting Minimalist Habits for Personal Wellness

Clutter doesn't just crowd your physical space - it contributes to mental stress too. Decision fatigue sets in because every item demands your attention or decision making in some way – whether it's where to store it or how often you need to clean it.

By decluttering and simplifying, you're creating an environment that fosters calmness and focus. You're also freeing up time - time otherwise spent cleaning or organizing - to invest in activities that nourish your wellbeing.

Creating a Minimalist Haven

To start your minimalist journey, begin by decluttering one room at a time. Decide on the items that enhance your life and those that don't.

Donate, sell, or responsibly dispose of things you no longer need.

When purchasing new items, consider their quality, sustainability, and versatility. Buying less but better reduces waste and saves you money in the long run by minimizing the need for replacements.

And, very importantly, choose items that are less likely to pollute your indoor air environment. The United States Environmental Protection Agency has reported that indoor levels of volatile organic compounds (VOCs) are often 1,000-2,000 times higher than outdoor levels. What can you do about that?

Be practical. Consider tile or hardwood flooring with organic cotton throw rugs if necessary, rather than laminate flooring or wall-to-wall carpeting (you know how bad that chemical smell can be from new carpet and the backing materials). Consider finding real wood furniture or modernistic glass and metal items rather than the composite woods and compressed wood sawdust and glue furniture that is cheaper, but outgasses/off-gasses formaldehyde and other volatile organic compounds (VOCs). Even when you buy new clothes or bedding, air them outdoors or in a garage first for several days and/or wash them to remove the excess chemical treatments they may contain. For nursery furniture, look for items with a Greenguard certification that supports their lower risk of releasing VOCs into your child's air.

The Bottom Line: Embrace Minimalism for Healthier Living

It's critical to understand that adopting minimalism isn't about deprivation - it's about making space – physically and mentally – for what truly matters to you.

By reducing clutter and focusing on mindful consumption, you'll foster a healthier mindset while contributing positively to our planet. Remember Susan's transformation - let it inspire you as you begin on your own pathway towards minimalism.

Chapter 4: The Green Home Revolution

E mily, an ardent advocate of sustainability, had always dreamt of building her own eco-friendly home. After years of planning and saving, she finally got the opportunity to turn her dream into reality.

She started with a clear vision: a house that minimized it's environmental impact and promoted her family's health and well-being.

She invested in energy-efficient appliances, used natural building materials, and insisted on toxin-free interiors. It was a challenging journey at times but looking back, Emily wouldn't have it any other way.

Her home reduced their carbon footprint and improved their quality of life remarkably.

Just like Emily's experience shows us, creating a sustainable living space can be transformative for both the environment and our personal health. This chapter aims to guide you through understanding the importance of sustainable homes and offering actionable advice on how to create your own healthy living space.

Green Living Starts from Building Materials

When thinking about sustainability in architecture, consider starting from the very base - the building materials. Opting for sustainable materials such as reclaimed wood or recycled metal reduces waste and decreases demand for non-renewable resources.

A study by Yale University found that "construction with wood has a significantly lower environmental impact compared to steel or concrete."

By choosing environmentally friendly building materials like Emily did, you are making an investment in both your home's future and the planet's longevity.

Energy Efficiency: An Eco-Friendly Investment

Investing in energy-efficient appliances is another crucial step towards creating a sustainable home. From LED lights to Energy Star-rated refrigerators, these products use less electricity which means lower utility bills and decreased greenhouse gas emissions.

The U.S Department of Energy states that "energy-efficient appliances reduce average household energy use by up to 30%," resulting in substantial savings over time as well as significant environmental benefits.

Toxin-Free Interiors for Healthier Homes

Switching to non-toxic paints and cleaning products is another essential aspect of creating a healthy living space. These products are free from harmful chemicals that can cause allergies, respiratory issues, and other health problems.

According to the Environmental Working Group, "cleaning supplies can be significant sources of indoor air pollution." Therefore, using toxin-free choices (including unscented products) contributes to a healthier home and improves your family's well-being.

Making the Most of Your Space: Air-Purifying Plants

If you don't have the luxury of a sprawling yard or abundant outdoor space like Emily did, fret not. Indoor plants can purify the air in your home while adding a touch of natural beauty.

Snake plants, spider plants, and ferns are just a few examples of indoor greenery that can help improve your home's air quality.

The Bottom Line: Building Towards Sustainability and Health

Creating a sustainable living space is more than just an eco-friendly initiative - it's an investment in your health and future. Like Emily's journey shows us, every step towards sustainability counts - whether it's opting for energy-efficient appliances or switching to non-toxic cleaning products.

Criteria for Choosing a Good Quality Room Air Purifier: Creating a Healthy Indoor Air Environment

Did you know that most people spend about 90% of their time indoors? Whether it's at home, in the office, or inside other buildings, we are breathing in indoor air far more than we realize. Unfortunately, the air inside can sometimes be even more polluted than the air outside due to trapped dust, mold spores, chemicals from cleaning products, and allergens. That's why improving indoor air quality is essential for maintaining good health, especially for those with respiratory issues or allergies.

One of the best ways to clean up indoor air is by using a high-quality air purifier. But not all air purifiers are created equal, so it's important to know what to look for when choosing the right one for your home. First, consider the room size. Air purifiers are rated for the amount of square footage they can effectively clean. You'll want to make sure the air purifier is strong enough to cover the size of the room where it will be used. For example, a purifier rated for 300 square feet may work well in a bedroom, but may not be powerful enough for a large living room.

Another key feature is the fan noise level. While it may seem like a minor detail, fan noise can become a nuisance if the purifier runs all day or while you're trying to sleep. Look for models with quieter settings or fan speeds that can be adjusted to a comfortable level without sacrificing air cleaning power.

When it comes to the types of pollutants the purifier can remove, the most important factor is having a HEPA filter stage. HEPA filters are designed to capture very small particles, including dust, pollen, pet dander, and even viruses and mold spores. These particles can irritate the lungs and contribute to health issues like asthma or allergies. For even better protection, some air purifiers also come with activated carbon filters, which are great for removing chemical pollutants, odors, and volatile organic compounds (VOCs) that come from things like cleaning products, furniture, and paint.

A HEPA filter is crucial because it can trap airborne pollutants as small as 0.3 microns, effectively removing harmful particles that can cause respiratory problems. This feature is especially important for households with young children, the elderly, or anyone with existing health issues. Having an air purifier with both a HEPA filter and an activated carbon filter can dramatically improve your indoor air quality, making your home a healthier place to live.

***

By understanding these elements and implementing the advice laid out in this chapter, you will confirm that your home becomes an epitome of green living - one that fosters good health as much as it champions environmental preservation.

Chapter 5: The Eco-Friendly Wardrobe: Sustainable Fashion and Personal Wellness

Amanda, a fashion enthusiast, was constantly updating her wardrobe with the latest trends. She loved the thrill of snagging a good deal on fast-fashion websites.

However, over time, Amanda began to notice the fleeting lifespan of these clothes.

They quickly wore out or fell out of style.

One day, Amanda stumbled upon an article detailing the environmental impact of fast fashion. It spoke about how this industry contributes significantly to global pollution and wastes colossal amounts of water.

The article also mentioned that synthetic fabrics and chemical dyes could cause skin irritations and allergies.

Shaken by these revelations, Amanda made a conscious decision - she chose to transform her wardrobe into one that was sustainable and eco-friendly.

Just like Amanda, you too can make a significant positive impact on your health and the environment by embracing sustainable fashion. This chapter will guide you through understanding what it means to have an eco-friendly wardrobe and offer practical advice on making this transformation.

Understanding Fast Fashion's Environmental Impact

Fast fashion refers to inexpensive clothing produced rapidly by mass-market retailers in response to current trends. While this may seem like an economical choice for many consumers, it has severe environmental repercussions.

According to a study by Ellen MacArthur Foundation, "the equivalent of one garbage truck full of clothes is burned or dumped in a landfill every second."

Your decision to opt for sustainable clothing can play a part in reducing this alarming statistic.

Building A Sustainable Wardrobe

Sustainable fashion involves choosing quality over quantity. Instead of buying many cheap items that won't last long, invest in timeless pieces made from natural materials such as cotton or linen. Natural silk is a good choice too.

These fabrics are durable and kinder to your skin compared to synthetic alternatives. If you start noticing rashes or skin irritation, ask yourself if you changed laundry detergents – or did you start wearing some newer clothing item that you haven't outgassed or washed before putting it on.

Supporting Ethical Brands

Ethical brands prioritize fair trade practices and confirm their workers are paid fairly while maintaining environmentally friendly production processes. When shopping for new pieces for your wardrobe, consider brands that align with these values. Certainly look for organic cotton options for clothes and bedding.

Embracing Secondhand Shopping

Secondhand shopping is a fantastic way to reduce waste and find unique pieces at affordable prices. Consider exploring local thrift shops or online platforms that offer pre-loved clothes.

Creating A Capsule Wardrobe

A capsule wardrobe comprises a small collection of versatile items that can be mixed and matched to create numerous outfits. This approach reduces decision fatigue and promotes minimalism, which has been linked to reduced stress levels according to a study in the Journal of Happiness Studies.

The Bottom Line: Sustainable Fashion For A Healthy You And Planet

Choosing sustainable fashion is about more than just reducing your carbon footprint - this involves promoting personal wellness and making informed decisions that reflect your values.

By embracing the practical advice outlined in this chapter, you can improve your wardrobe into an eco-friendly one, improving both your health and the environment — just like Amanda.

Chapter 6: Transportation Choices: How to Drive Down Your Carbon Footprint

Overview: Explore the environmental and health benefits of eco-friendly transportation options, including cycling, walking, electric vehicles, and public transportation.

Key Topics: Carpooling, public transit, electric vehicles, biking, walking.

Health Connection: Show how walking and cycling promote physical fitness, reduce stress, and improve cardiovascular health, while also lowering carbon emissions.

Action Steps: Encourage readers to reduce their reliance on cars, explore electric or hybrid vehicle options, or commit to walking and biking more frequently.

Every morning, Jane would dutifully climb into her SUV and join the throng of vehicles inching their way towards the city center. The daily grind of traffic, noise, and exhaust fumes was a frustrating routine that she accepted as a necessary part of city living.

One particular morning, amid the usual chaos on the freeway, Jane noticed a group of cyclists breezing past the gridlocked cars. She watched as they moved freely and easily through the city streets.

Intrigued by this alternative mode of commuting, Jane decided to swap her car keys for a bicycle helmet.

The change wasn't easy at first - she had to navigate bike lanes and deal with unpredictable weather conditions. But soon, she began enjoying her commute - it became an opportunity for exercise and fresh air rather than a source of stress.

More importantly, Jane realized that by cycling instead of driving, she was significantly reducing her carbon footprint.

If you're like Jane and looking for ways to make your transportation choices more eco-friendly while also benefiting your health, then this chapter is for you.

Understanding Your Transportation Footprint

Transportation accounts for nearly 30% of greenhouse gas emissions in the United States alone. The combustion engines in traditional cars release harmful gases such as carbon dioxide (CO_2), methane (CH_4), and nitrous oxide (N_2O) into the atmosphere.

These are all significant contributors to climate change.

By making conscious choices about how we travel - be it commuting to work or running errands - we can play our part in reducing these emissions.

Throw in some Pedal Power

Cycling is great cardio but it's also one of the most sustainable modes of transportation available. According to research published in Environmental Health Perspectives, "Bicycling just 5 miles each way to work instead of driving could reduce an average person's household emissions by about 8%."

Plus, cycling improves cardiovascular fitness while burning calories and reducing stress. It's a win-win for your health and the environment.

Embrace Electric Vehicles

If biking or walking isn't an option due to distance or physical limitations, consider switching to an electric vehicle (EV). EVs are gaining popularity as a cleaner alternative to traditional gas-powered vehicles. Yes, there are more and more electric vehicles going on the market every year. That may be another strategy as prices come down to levels competitive with gas-powered cars and trucks.

According to the U.S.

Department of Energy, "Electric vehicles convert about 59%–62% of the electrical energy from the grid to power at the wheels—conventional gasoline vehicles only convert about 17%–21% of the energy stored in gasoline." That is, you can get more transportation with EVs than with gas-powered vehicles.

The Bottom Line: Choose Sustainable Transportation

Reducing your carbon footprint doesn't mean you have to give up mobility. By opting for sustainable transportation options like cycling, walking, carpooling, or driving electric vehicles, you can significantly reduce your emissions while also reaping health benefits.

Like Jane, you too can improve your daily commute into an opportunity for exercise and environmental stewardship. By understanding and implementing these eco-friendly transportation choices, you'll contribute positively towards tackling climate change and enjoy a healthier lifestyle.

What's the use of a fine house if you haven't got a tolerable planet to put it on?" - Henry David Thoreau

Chapter 7: Reducing Waste: How to Embrace Zero Waste Living for Better Health

Jane, a busy executive, found herself increasingly concerned about the stacks of plastic containers and take-out boxes that filled her trash each week. She began feeling overwhelmed not just by the clutter in her home and by the thought of her contribution to the growing waste problem.

One day, Jane decided to make a change. She started small, carrying reusable shopping bags and refusing single-use plastics.

Gradually, she adopted composting and focused on buying items with minimal packaging.

Over time, she noticed changes - not just in her shrinking waste bin and in her health and well-being.

Embracing zero-waste living helped Jane declutter her life, reduce exposure to harmful chemicals often found in plastics, and contribute positively towards reducing environmental pollution.

Just like Jane, you too can adopt a zero-waste lifestyle for better health and a cleaner environment. This chapter will guide you through understanding the importance of reducing waste and provide practical advice on how to start the effort you put in towards zero waste living.

"Understanding Your Trash: The First Step Towards Zero-Waste"

The first step towards reducing your waste is understanding what constitutes it. Start by analyzing what goes into your trash bin each week – food scraps?

Plastic wrappers?

Disposable cups?

A study published by Environmental Science & Technology notes that "the average American throws away approximately 4.4 pounds (2 kg) of trash every day."

By analyzing your trash patterns, you can identify areas where you can minimize waste production.

"Refuse, Reduce, Reuse: The Three Rs of Zero-Waste Living"

Adopting the three Rs - Refuse, Reduce and Reuse - is crucial in embarking on your zero-waste journey.

When possible refuse unnecessary items such as plastic straws or promotional freebies that might end up as clutter or landfill fodder. Try something simple – e.g., reusable stainless steel straws instead.

Reduce consumption wherever possible - for example, buy in bulk instead of individually packaged items.

Reuse what you have rather than opting for disposable alternatives. For instance, use a refillable water bottle made with BPA-free plastic, stainless steel, or glass instead of buying single-use plastic bottles.

"Recycling and Composting: Turning Trash into Treasure"

Recycling is the process of converting waste materials into reusable objects to prevent waste of potentially useful materials. Make use of your local recycling programs for items like paper, glass, and metal.

Composting, on the other hand, is nature's process of recycling decomposed organic materials into a rich soil known as compost. It's a great way to reduce food waste and enrich your garden soil.

The Bottom Line: Embrace Zero Waste Living

Embracing zero-waste living isn't about reducing landfill contribution - it's also about creating healthier living environments by reducing exposure to harmful chemicals often found in plastics and disposables.

As with Jane's experience, adopting a zero-waste lifestyle can lead to positive changes in your health and well-being while making a meaningful contribution towards environmental conservation.

By understanding your trash patterns and implementing the practical advice outlined in this chapter - refusing unnecessary items, reducing consumption, reusing resources, recycling suitable items and composting organic waste - you will be well on your way towards embracing a healthier zero-waste lifestyle.

Chapter 8: "Water Conservation: The Key to a Healthy Planet and You"

In the heart of Los Angeles, Mary Smith lived in a traditional suburban home. Like many others, she never gave much thought to her water usage - until one scorching summer.

That year, California was hit by one of it's most severe droughts in history.

Mary noticed her lush green lawn turning brown and wilting. Her once vibrant roses were drooping and parched.

It wasn't just her garden that suffered - the water restrictions imposed during the drought made Mary realize how much she took clean, accessible water for granted.

Motivated to make a change for herself and for her planet, Mary began implementing strategies to conserve water within her household. What started as small changes like fixing leaks and using efficient appliances soon transformed into larger initiatives like installing rainwater harvesting systems and recycling greywater.

Like Mary's eye-opening experience, this chapter aims to highlight the importance of water conservation for both our planet's health and our own well-being.

"Understanding Your Water Footprint"

Water is an essential resource that we use every day without second thought. However, it's worth noting that the average American family uses more than 300 gallons of water per day at home.

It's important to understand your "water footprint," which includes direct consumption from household uses such as drinking or showering and indirect consumption related to food production or energy usage.

A report by Water Research Foundation states that "households can reduce their direct indoor water use by about 35% if they adopt efficient fixtures and appliances."

"Making Playful Changes: Reducing Water Usage"

Reducing your household's water usage doesn't have to be a tiresome chore - it can actually be quite fun! Simple changes such as turning off taps while brushing teeth or washing hands, taking shorter showers, or using a dishwasher instead of hand-washing dishes can make a significant difference.

The United States Environmental Protection Agency suggests that "using a dishwasher instead of hand-washing dishes uses less water and saves the homeowner nearly 230 hours per year."

"Rainwater Harvesting and Greywater Systems"

Rainwater harvesting is an excellent way to use natural resources while reducing reliance on municipal water. By installing a rainwater collection system, you can capture and store rainwater for various non-drinking uses such as watering plants or flushing toilets. You can find many different choices online or locally.

Meanwhile, recycling greywater—water from baths, sinks, washing machines, and other kitchen appliances—can further reduce your water footprint. Greywater can be reused for purposes like irrigation or toilet flushing.

A study published in the Journal of Cleaner Production found that "rainwater harvesting could reduce household water consumption by up to 50%, while greywater reuse could save up to 30%."

"The Bottom Line: Water Conservation is Everyone's Responsibility"

Like Mary Smith uncovered during California's drought season, conserving water is not about surviving extreme weather—it's about ensuring the health of our planet and ourselves.

Water conservation strategies can significantly reduce your household's environmental impact while also fostering a deeper appreciation for this vital resource.

By understanding the importance of saving water and implementing practical solutions outlined in this chapter, you'll contribute to preserving clean, accessible water for future generations—and promote your own health along the way. Just like Mary did.

And if chemical pollution of your showering and/or drinking water is a concern, look into ways to filter out the contaminants before they get into the water you use for bathing, cooking, and drinking. For that purpose, there are whole house water filters with activated carbon filters as well as widely-available water filter attachments for your kitchen and bathroom faucets and showers. Remove the chlorine and fluoride, lead and other heavy metals with guidance from a water purification expert. Be aware that water softeners do not filter out chemical contaminants.

Of course, even most of the bottled waters out there are going to contaminate their contents with plastics. Sometimes water filtration straws may help – but check them out in detail before buying. Your best bet is probably to buy bottled waters when you do want or need them, in glass bottles. And carry around your water supplies in BPA-free plastics or, even better, stainless steel containers.

Chapter 9: Harnessing the Importance of Sustainable Energy

Oliver, a high school science teacher, was always passionate about educating his students about environmental conservation. He believed in leading by example and was determined to transform his lifestyle into a more sustainable one.

His first project?

Switching over to renewable energy.

He started with installing solar panels on the roof of his suburban home. The initial investment was steep, but Oliver saw it as an investment for the future.

Slowly, he began to see changes – both in his electricity bills and the environment around him.

His carbon footprint reduced significantly, the air felt cleaner, and he noticed a subtle shift in his overall health. This substantial transformation sparked an enlightening realization about the power of renewable energy sources.

Just like Oliver's experience, this chapter will guide you through understanding various renewable energy sources like solar, wind, and geothermal energy. It will help you comprehend their benefits on both your personal health and our planet's health while offering practical ways to incorporate them into your life.

"Understanding Solar Energy"

Harnessing solar energy is about utilizing one of nature's most abundant resources - sunlight. As Jonathan Swift wisely stated: "A light heart lives long." And indeed, light can provide longevity not just for us humans and for our planet.

Solar panels installed on rooftops can generate enough electricity to power an entire household. They are cost-efficient in the long run and reduce dependence on fossil fuels drastically.

According to National Renewable Energy Laboratory (NREL), residential solar panels can offset nearly 100% of household electricity use with clean energy from the sun."

"Wind Energy: An Invisible Force"

Harnessing wind power involves using turbines that convert kinetic energy from wind into mechanical power or electricity. Wind farms are increasingly becoming common sights across landscapes worldwide because of their efficiency and sustainability.

The American Wind Energy Association noted that "a single wind turbine can generate enough electricity to power 500 homes."

"Geothermal Energy: The Heat Beneath Us"

Geothermal energy uses the Earth's natural heat to generate electricity or heat homes. It is a reliable and constant source of power, unlike solar and wind energy that depend on weather conditions.

A study by Stanford University revealed that "geothermal energy could supply America with more than 10% of it's electricity needs, all while producing virtually no pollution."

"The Bottom Line: Making the Green Switch"

Transitioning to sustainable energy sources is not just an environmental necessity and a health imperative. Cleaner energy means cleaner air, leading to fewer respiratory and cardiovascular diseases. And outdoors around your home and garden, get solar-powered lighting. It will pay you back with cost savings on your electric bill and shift you into having a more sustainable modern home.

And if you are into hiking and camping – or preparing for surviving natural disasters with the many challenges that arise every year, see about getting some solar-powered devices like emergency radios, lanterns, flashlights, and generators,

It may seem daunting at first, like Oliver's initial journey into renewable energy. But remember - every little step counts towards making our planet healthier and our future brighter.

By understanding these renewable resources and incorporating them in your life, you'll contribute significantly to reducing carbon emissions and promoting cleaner air, just like Oliver did.

From an industry expert:"Investing in renewable energy creates jobs, reduces emissions and drives economic growth"- Adnan Z

Amin, Director-General International Renewable Energy Agency (IRENA).

Chapter 10: Dealing with EMF Exposures in Your Environment

What Are EMFs?

Electromagnetic fields (EMFs) are invisible areas of energy that come from electronic devices like cell phones, computers, Wi-Fi routers, microwaves, and power lines. While we rely on many of these devices in our daily lives, concerns have been raised about how constant exposure to EMFs may affect our health. Some people report feeling symptoms like headaches, fatigue, and difficulty concentrating when they are exposed to high levels of EMFs, while others worry about long-term health risks.

Although the research is still ongoing, and scientists have not yet reached a full consensus on the dangers of EMF exposure, it's a good idea to take precautions—especially since we are surrounded by so many sources of EMFs in modern life.

Even though the health effects of EMF exposure are still being studied, some researchers suggest that long-term exposure could be linked to several health issues. These include:

- **Sleep disturbances**: Some people find it harder to fall asleep or stay asleep when exposed to high levels of EMFs, especially from devices like cell phones or Wi-Fi routers placed near the bed.

- **Headaches and fatigue**: EMF exposure has been reported to cause headaches, dizziness, and feelings of tiredness in people who are more sensitive to electromagnetic energy.

- **Increased risk of certain cancers**: There is ongoing debate about whether long-term exposure to EMFs, especially from cell phones, may increase the risk of certain cancers, such as brain tumors.

- **Potential links to fertility issues**: Some studies have suggested that exposure to EMFs could affect sperm quality in men and may play a role in fertility problems.

While more research is needed to confirm these risks, reducing your exposure to EMFs can be a simple way to take control of your environment and protect your health.

***

Steps to Reduce EMF Exposure at Home

1. Limit Your Use of Electronic Devices

- One of the easiest ways to reduce your exposure to EMFs is to use electronic devices less frequently, especially those that emit higher levels of electromagnetic energy, like cell phones, laptops, and tablets. Whenever possible, try to take regular breaks from screen time and use devices only when necessary.

- **Tip**: If you're on a phone call, use speaker mode or a hands-free headset to keep your phone away from your head and reduce EMF exposure.

2. Create an EMF-Free Sleep Zone

- Sleep is a time for your body to recharge, so it's important to keep your sleep environment as free from EMFs as possible. Avoid keeping cell phones, tablets, or laptops near your bed, and consider turning off your Wi-Fi router at night.

- **Tip**: If you use an alarm clock, choose a battery-powered one instead of an electric one that plugs into the wall.

3. Use Wired Connections Instead of Wireless

- Many of the devices we use today rely on wireless signals, like Wi-Fi, Bluetooth, and cellular data, which all emit EMFs. By using wired connections instead, you can significantly reduce the amount of EMFs in your home. For example, you can switch from Wi-Fi to Ethernet cables for your internet connection or use wired headphones instead of Bluetooth ones.

- **Tip**: If you need to use Wi-Fi, place the router as far away from common living spaces and bedrooms as possible to limit exposure.

4. Turn Off Devices When Not in Use

- Electronics like TVs, computers, and gaming consoles often remain on standby mode even when you're not using them, meaning they continue to emit EMFs. Make a habit of turning off and unplugging these devices when they're not in use.

- **Tip**: Use a power strip for multiple electronics so you can easily turn off several devices at once.

5. Create Distance from EMF Sources

- The strength of EMFs decreases with distance, so one of the best ways to reduce your exposure is to simply move farther away from the source. For example, try not to carry your phone in your pocket all day or sit too close to your computer screen.

- **Tip**: Keep your cell phone or tablet in a bag or on a desk, rather than in your hand or lap, to reduce direct exposure.

6. Use EMF Shielding Products

- There are products on the market designed to block or reduce EMF exposure, such as EMF-blocking phone cases, laptop shields, and special fabrics for clothing or bedding. While the effectiveness of these products can vary, they may provide some additional protection if you're particularly concerned about EMF exposure.

- **Tip**: Look for reputable companies that provide research or testing results to back up the effectiveness of their EMF-shielding products.

7. Reduce Smart Device Usage

- Many modern homes are filled with "smart" devices like smart speakers, smart thermostats, and smart TVs, all of which connect wirelessly to the internet and increase EMF exposure. Consider whether these devices are necessary in your home, and turn off their wireless functions when they're not in use.

- **Tip**: Disable Bluetooth and Wi-Fi on your smart devices when they are not being used to reduce EMF emissions.

***

Final Thoughts on EMF Exposure

While we may not be able to completely avoid EMF exposure in our daily lives, taking simple steps to reduce it can help create a healthier living environment for you and your family. By limiting the use of electronic devices, creating an EMF-free sleep zone, and turning off devices when they're not in use, you can cut down on unnecessary exposure to electromagnetic energy.

Remember, being aware of your surroundings and making small changes to your habits can go a long way toward creating a safer, more balanced environment—both for your well-being and for the planet.

Chapter 11: Light Pollution and Its Effects on Sleep and Health

What Is Light Pollution?

Light pollution is the presence of artificial light in the environment at night. This can come from streetlights, car headlights, illuminated signs, or even the glow of electronic devices like TVs, phones, and computers. While artificial light helps us navigate the world after dark, too much exposure to it—especially at night—can mess with our natural sleep-wake cycles, also known as our circadian rhythm.

The human body is designed to follow the natural pattern of daylight and darkness. Our circadian rhythm tells us when it's time to be awake and when it's time to sleep. But with the constant presence of artificial light, especially blue light from screens, our bodies can get confused, which can lead to health problems.

How Light Pollution Affects Sleep and Health

When we're exposed to bright lights at night, it can interfere with the production of a hormone called **melatonin**. Melatonin helps regulate our sleep by making us feel sleepy when it's dark outside. But when we're exposed to artificial light in the evening, especially blue light from phones, tablets, and computers, melatonin production decreases. This can make it harder to fall asleep and stay asleep.

Here's how light pollution can affect our sleep and overall health:

- **Sleep Problems**: When our melatonin levels are too low, we have trouble falling asleep, wake up more during the night, and may not get the deep, restful sleep our bodies need. Poor sleep can lead to fatigue, irritability, and trouble concentrating during the day.

- **Disrupted Circadian Rhythm**: Light pollution can throw off our circadian rhythm, making it harder to wake up feeling refreshed and making us feel tired at odd times of the day.

- **Long-Term Health Risks**: Over time, poor sleep caused by light pollution can lead to more serious health problems like heart disease, diabetes, and depression. Studies have even linked long-term exposure to artificial light at night with an increased risk of cancer, especially breast cancer, because of the way it interferes with melatonin production.

Simple Steps to Get Back in Harmony with Natural Light-Dark Cycles

The good news is that you can take steps to reduce your exposure to light pollution and get your sleep back on track. Here are some simple tips to help you sync up with the natural light-dark cycle and improve your sleep and health.

1. Dim the Lights in the Evening

One of the easiest ways to reduce light pollution in your home is to dim the lights as the evening progresses. This helps signal to your body that it's time to wind down and get ready for sleep.

- **Tip**: Use lamps with low-watt bulbs in the evening instead of overhead lights, and consider using dimmable light switches or smart lights that can automatically reduce brightness at night.

- **Bonus**: Candles or soft, warm lighting can create a cozy atmosphere without interfering with your melatonin levels.

2. Limit Screen Time Before Bed

Blue light from electronic devices is one of the biggest culprits when it comes to disrupting sleep. Phones, computers, and tablets all emit blue light, which can trick your brain into thinking it's still daytime, making it harder to fall asleep.

- **Tip**: Try to avoid using screens at least one hour before bedtime. If you have to use your phone or computer in the evening, consider installing a blue light filter app or using the device's built-in "night mode" to reduce blue light exposure.

- **Bonus**: Replace screen time before bed with a relaxing activity like reading a book, doing some light stretching, or practicing meditation.

3. Use Blackout Curtains or Sleep Masks

If you live in an area with a lot of outdoor lighting—like streetlights or traffic—it's a good idea to block out as much of that light as possible in your bedroom. Too much light in the room, even if it's coming from outside, can keep you from falling asleep or staying asleep through the night.

- **Tip**: Install blackout curtains in your bedroom to keep out unwanted light, or use a silk sleep mask if blackout curtains aren't an option.

- **Bonus**: If you need a little light to move around at night, use a red or amber night light. These colors are less likely to disrupt your melatonin production compared to regular white or blue light.

4. Get More Natural Light During the Day

Exposure to natural sunlight during the day helps keep your circadian rhythm in check. When you get enough sunlight in the morning and early afternoon, it signals to your body that it's time to be awake and alert, which helps you feel more tired when it's time to sleep at night.

- **Tip**: Try to spend at least 15–30 minutes outside each day, especially in the morning, to boost your exposure to natural light. If you can't get outside, sit by a window where you can get some sunlight.

- **Bonus**: Going for a short walk outside during the day not only helps with sleep but also boosts your mood and energy levels.

5. Turn Off or Block Electronics in the Bedroom

Many electronics, like alarm clocks, TVs, or even Wi-Fi routers, give off small amounts of light that can interfere with your sleep. These little lights might not seem like a big deal, but they can be enough to disrupt your body's ability to stay in sync with the natural light-dark cycle.

- **Tip**: Remove as many electronic devices from your bedroom as possible, or at least turn off the ones that have lights. If you can't turn them off, cover the light with electrical tape or cloth to block it out.

- **Bonus**: Keep your phone charging in another room to avoid the temptation to check it in the middle of the night, and use a traditional alarm clock that doesn't emit bright light.

6. Create a Sleep-Friendly Environment

The more relaxing and calming your bedroom is, the easier it will be to fall asleep and stay asleep. Reducing light pollution is an important part of creating a sleep-friendly environment, but other factors like temperature, noise, and overall comfort also play a role.

- **Tip**: Keep your bedroom cool, quiet, and dark to promote better sleep. Invest in comfortable bedding and make your sleep space as restful as possible.

- **Bonus**: Try using calming scents like lavender or chamomile, which are known for their sleep-promoting effects.

Final Thoughts on Light Pollution and Sleep

Light pollution is all around us, but with a few small changes, you can reduce its impact on your sleep and overall health. By limiting your exposure to artificial light at night and embracing more natural light during the day, you can help your body get back in sync with the natural rhythms of light and dark. This simple shift can lead to better sleep, improved energy, and a healthier, happier life.

Strive to live in harmony with your environment indoors and outdoors.

Exposure to green space reduces stress and improves physical and mental wellbeing" – Environmental Science & Technology Journal

Tip: *Plant trees or create green spaces around your home for better air quality.*

Chapter 12 Mindful Travel: How to Explore the World Sustainably

Oliver, a seasoned traveler, had always loved the thrill of exploring new places. He would jump from one city to another in record time, trying to cover as many tourist spots as possible.

However, over time, he started realizing that his fast-paced travels were leaving him more exhausted than enriched.

One day while browsing through a travel blog, Oliver stumbled upon the concept of "mindful travel." Intrigued by the idea of slow and sustainable tourism, he decided to plan his next trip differently.

For his next adventure, he chose a small coastal town known for it's sustainable practices and rich culture. Instead of cramming multiple activities into each day, he spent time appreciating the beauty around him and engaging with locals.

He ditched his habit of relying on planes for every move and instead used local transportation or cycled wherever possible.

The difference was astounding. Oliver returned from this trip feeling rejuvenated and enriched with heartfelt experiences and newfound respect for nature.

His transformation highlighted the importance of mindful travel - a concept that benefits our planet and adds depth to our adventures.

Just like Oliver's experience taught him about mindful travel's transformative power, this chapter will guide you through understanding it's significance and offering practical advice on how to explore the world sustainably.

"Sustainable Travel: What Does It Mean?"

Sustainable travel encourages minimizing environmental impact while maximizing cultural appreciation and personal growth. The United Nations World Tourism Organization defines Sustainable Tourism as "tourism that takes full account of its current and future economic, social and environmental impacts."

It's not just about preserving nature - this involves contributing positively towards your destination's economy by supporting local businesses. It's also about immersing yourself in the culture as opposed to observing it from afar.

"Slow Travel: A Key Component"

The philosophy behind slow travel is simple: take your time to engage deeply with your surroundings as opposed to hurrying through them. As author Pico Iyer said, "In an age of acceleration, nothing can be more exhilarating than going slow."

"Choosing Sustainable Transport"

Transportation is one of the most significant contributors to a traveler's carbon footprint. Consider using public transportation, cycling, or walking when possible.

If flying is necessary, consider purchasing carbon offsets to neutralize the environmental impact.

"Sustainable Accommodations and Local Eateries"

Choose accommodations that prioritize sustainable practices such as water conservation, recycling, and energy efficiency. Similarly, eating at local eateries supports the local economy and reduces the carbon footprint associated with shipping food over long distances.

The Bottom Line: Embrace Mindful Travel

If Oliver's transformation has taught us anything, it's that mindful travel isn't about decreasing our environmental impact - it's also about enhancing our travel experiences.

By understanding what mindful travel entails and implementing the practical advice outlined in this chapter, you can enrich your travel experiences while making positive contributions to our planet. Like Oliver, you may find yourself returning from your trips feeling not just refreshed and enriched by deeper cultural insights and a greater appreciation for nature.

Conclusion: Your Green Journey Begins Here

For years, Sarah had lived a hectic city life, always in pursuit of the next big thing. Her days were filled with endless meetings, hurried meals and instant gratification purchases.

However, when she decided to take a breather and escape to her grandmother's countryside cottage for the weekend, little did she know that it would change her perspective on life.

Sarah was entranced by the simplicity of her grandmother's lifestyle - using fresh produce from the garden for meals, recycling every possible item, minimizing waste and living in harmony with nature. She realized that such a lifestyle benefited the environment and fostered better health and well-being.

Inspired to make a change in her own life, Sarah returned to the city with renewed vigor. She started making conscious choices about her consumption habits, invested time in understanding where her food came from and made an effort to reduce waste.

Her journey towards sustainable living had begun.

Much like Sarah's experience, your progress toward sustainable living can begin at any point in your life. This chapter will provide you with practical advice on how you can get started on this path while improving both your personal health and wellbeing.

"Green Living: A Personal Choice"

Choosing sustainability is more than just an environmental choice - it's a personal one too. It's about understanding that our actions have consequences beyond ourselves.

Just as we need adequate exercise for our bodies or nourishing food for our health, we need sustainable practices to confirm the health of our planet. Start small – try walking or cycling instead of driving short distances or consider bringing reusable bags when you shop.

A study by The Lancet Commission has found that "policies aimed at combating climate change could save millions of lives because of healthier diets."

The benefits clearly extend beyond saving the planet – they contribute directly to your personal health too!

"Playing Your Part: Reducing Waste"

One effective way of embracing sustainability is by reducing waste. This includes physical waste, like food and packaging, as well as intangible waste, such as energy.

Invest in reusable items to cut down on single-use products. Practice mindful consumption – only buy what you need and will use.

Turn off lights when leaving a room and unplug devices when they are not in use.

As per a study from Stanford University, "Americans throw away 25 percent more trash during the Thanksgiving to New Year's holiday period than any other time of year."

By adopting more sustainable practices, can you contribute towards reducing this figure and save money in the process.

"Space Matters: Sustainable Living Spaces"

The spaces we live in play a huge role in our sustainability journey. An eco-friendly home reduces carbon footprint while promoting healthier living conditions.

Consider using natural light over artificial wherever possible or switching to energy-efficient appliances. Planting greenery indoors helps to improve air quality while adding aesthetic value.

A study published in Environmental Science & Technology has shown that "green buildings provide nearly 30% savings in energy use compared to non-green buildings."

This goes beyond just monetary saving – it directly contributes towards preserving our environment for future generations.

"The Bottom Line: Every Choice Counts"

Every step taken towards sustainable living counts. Remember that this isn't an all-or-nothing endeavor - even small changes can have a big impact.

It's about understanding that every choice we make can either contribute to the problem or be part of the solution. It's about realizing that sustainable living is not just beneficial for our planet but for our personal health too.

Just like Sarah, begin your path today and watch how these small steps lead to significant improvements both personally and globally.

"One individual cannot possibly make a difference alone - it is individual efforts, collectively, that makes a noticeable difference." - Dr.Jane Goodall

About the Author - Dr. Iris Bell

Dr. Iris R. Bell, MD PhD is an internationally-recognized researcher, educator, and consultant who has focused her work on environmental health and complementary medicine. She is a retired professor at the University of Arizona College of Medicine who has been honored in both the conventional medical world with listings in *The Best Doctors in America* and the homeopathic world with the *CF Samuel Hahnemann Educator Award* from the American Institute of Homeopathy and the *Peter Fisher Memorial Award* from the National Center for Homeopathy.

A Board-certified psychiatrist and psychophysiology researcher, she has studied various areas of complementary and alternative medicine over the course of her career. She is certified in biofeedback (Biofeedback Certification Institute of America), a fellow of the American College of Nutrition, and a licensed homeopathic and allopathic (conventional) physician in Arizona. Dr. Bell has published over 150 peer-reviewed articles, a dozen book chapters, and a monograph on environmental chemical sensitivity.

Her current research interests revolve around synthesizing complexity science and homeopathic theory in understanding the healing process at the whole person level of organization. Her integrative healthcare book for the consumer on how to integrate multiple holistic therapies including mind-body therapies, nutritional supplements, herbs, acupuncture, and homeopathy is entitled *Getting Whole, Getting Well: Healing Holistically from Chronic Illness.*

Her main website is at https://dririsbell.com.

Claim your FREE copies of guides, checklists, cheat sheets, and more below at...

Brain Boosting Natural Remedies Cheat Sheet Offer – https://www.dririsbell.com/top-natural-brain-remedies-offer

Toxin-Free Blueprint – https://www.dynamicselfcare.com/toxin-free-living-blueprint-offer

Natural Remedies for Stress and Anxiety- https://www.dririsbell.com/natural-remedies-for-stress-and-anxiety

Please post a review you write on the bookseller vendor site where you got it and/or on GoodReads.com or on Bookbub.com.

When you are posting an Amazon review, go to the Amazon book page and scroll down the the **left side of the page** past the About the Author section until you arrive at Customer Reviews. There is often a button there for you to post a review of the product. If you are an ARC Team reader and received a free advance copy of the book, please state this information in your post.

Thanks again for reading my book!

Appendix

Scientific Studies

Here is a detailed list of scientific studies and sources that support the need for cleaning up both personal/family environments and the planetary environment. These studies cover a range of health and environmental impacts, from air pollution to toxins in food and everyday products.

1. Indoor Air Pollution and Health Risks

- **Study**: *The Burden of Disease from Indo or Air Pollution in Developing Countries: Comparison of Estimates*

  - **Citation**: Smith, K. R. (2000). *Environmental Health Perspectives*, 108(1), 481-488.

  - **Key Findings**: This study highlights the significant impact of indoor air pollution on health, especially respiratory conditions like asthma and lung infections. It calls for improved indoor air quality to prevent health problems.

- ○ **Relevance**: Demonstrates the importance of improving air quality in the home to protect personal and family health.

- **Link**: <u>Link to study</u>

2. Air Purifiers and Respiratory Health

- **Study**: *The Effect of Portable Air Cleaners on Asthma Control: A Randomized Controlled Trial*

  - ○ **Citation**: Sublett, J. L. et al. (2013). *Journal of Allergy and Clinical Immunology*, 131(1), 296-304.

  - ○ **Key Findings**: The use of air purifiers equipped with HEPA filters significantly reduced asthma symptoms in children exposed to particulate matter and allergens in indoor air.

  - ○ **Relevance**: Supports the use of air purifiers to improve indoor air quality and reduce the health burden of asthma, particularly in vulnerable populations like children.

- **Link**: Link to study

3. Environmental Toxins and Autism Risk

- **Study**: *Prenatal Exposure to Air Pollution and Risk of Autism Spectrum Disorders*

    ○ **Citation**: Volk, H. E., et al. (2013). *JAMA Psychiatry*, 70(1), 71-77.

    ○ **Key Findings**: This study found that exposure to traffic-related air pollution during pregnancy increases the risk of a child developing autism spectrum disorders.

    ○ **Relevance**: Highlights the importance of reducing exposure to pollutants, especially during critical developmental periods like pregnancy.

- **Link**: Link to study

4. Pesticides and Cancer Risk

- **Study**: *Pesticide Exposure and Cancer Incidence in the Agricultural Health Study*

    ○ **Citation**: Alavanja, M. C. R., et al. (2013). *Environmental Health Perspectives*, 121(8), 984-990.

    ○ **Key Findings**: The study links long-term pesticide exposure to an increased risk of cancers, including non-Hodgkin lymphoma and leukemia, among agricultural workers.

- ○ **Relevance**: Provides evidence of the need to reduce pesticide use and switch to organic food to lower cancer risks.

- **Link**: <u>Link to study</u>

5. Environmental Exposure to Heavy Metals and Neurodegenerative Diseases

- **Study**: *Chronic Exposure to Lead and the Risk of Parkinson's Disease*

  - ○ **Citation**: Weisskopf, M. G., et al. (2010). *Environmental Health Perspectives*, 118(11), 1609-1613.

  - ○ **Key Findings**: This study found a significant association between long-term lead exposure and the risk of developing Parkinson's disease, suggesting that heavy metals play a role in neurodegenerative diseases.

  - ○ **Relevance**: Supports efforts to reduce exposure to heavy metals like lead and mercury in everyday environments.

- **Link**: <u>Link to study</u>

6. Air Pollution and Cardiovascular Disease

- **Study**: *Air Pollution and Cardiovascular Disease: A Statement for Healthcare Professionals from the Expert Panel on Population and Prevention Science of the American Heart Association*

  - **Citation**: Brook, R. D., et al. (2010). *Circulation,* 121(21), 2331-2378.

  - **Key Findings**: This comprehensive review of studies shows that exposure to air pollution is a major risk factor for cardiovascular diseases such as heart attacks and strokes.

  - **Relevance**: Emphasizes the need to reduce air pollution to protect cardiovascular health, both at an individual and planetary level.

- **Link**: Link to study

7. Indoor Air Pollution and Cognitive Decline

- **Study**: *Indoor Air Pollution and Cognitive Performance: A Study of Exposure to Particulate Matter (PM2.5) in Older Adults*

  - **Citation**: Power, M. C., et al. (2016). *Environmental*

Research, 151, 1-7.

- **Key Findings**: The study found that exposure to fine particulate matter indoors is associated with cognitive decline in older adults, suggesting that poor indoor air quality may increase the risk of dementia.

- **Relevance**: Reinforces the importance of improving indoor air quality to protect cognitive health, particularly in aging populations.

- **Link**: <u>Link to study</u>

8. Chemical Exposures and Autoimmune Diseases

- **Study**: *Environmental Chemical Exposures and Autoimmune Diseases*

  - **Citation**: Cooper, G. S., & Parks, C. G. (2004). *Current Opinion in Rheumatology*, 16(3), 309-315.

  - **Key Findings**: This review of scientific literature explores how exposure to environmental chemicals, such as pesticides, solvents, and heavy metals, may trigger autoimmune diseases like lupus and rheumatoid arthritis.

  - **Relevance**: Provides evidence of the need to minimize exposure to environmental toxins to reduce the risk of autoimmune disorders.

- See also Contributions of synthetic chemical to autoimmune disease development and occurrence Curr Environ Health Rep 2024: 11(2):128-144.

9. Climate Change and Public Health

- **Study**: *The Impacts of Climate Change on Human Health in the United States: A Scientific Assessment*

  - **Citation**: US Global Change Research Program (2016).

  - **Key Findings**: This report outlines the ways in which climate change impacts public health, including increased risks of heat-related illnesses, infectious diseases, and respiratory problems due to worsening air quality.

  - **Relevance**: Supports efforts to address climate change as a critical factor in improving both planetary and personal health.

- **Link**: Link to study

10. Multiple Chemical Sensitivity and Environmental Toxins

- **Study**: *Prevalence of Multiple Chemical Sensitivities: A Population-Based Study*

  - **Citation**: Caress, S. M., & Steinemann, A. C. (2004). *Journal of Occupational and Environmental Medicine, 46*(8), 847-856.

  - **Key Findings**: This study examines the prevalence of Multiple Chemical Sensitivity (MCS) in the general population and its connection to environmental toxins. It suggests that people exposed to common chemicals like those in cleaning products, fragrances, and pesticides are at higher risk of developing MCS.

  - **Relevance**: Highlights the importance of reducing exposure to everyday chemical pollutants to prevent MCS and other health complications.

- **Link**: Link to study

11. Consumer Education about Indoor Air Quality and Symptoms of Chemical Intolerance

Study: Does improving indoor air quality lessen symptoms associated with chemical intolerance?

Citation: Perales, R.B., Palmer, R.F., Rincon, R.,, Viramontes, J.N., Walker, T., Jaen, C.R., & Miller, C.S. (2022). *Prim Health Care Res Dev.* 23

Key Findings: This study explores the relationship between indoor air quality (IAQ) and chemical intolerance (CI) symptoms. Environmental house calls were conducted to assess indoor volatile organic compound (VOC) levels and make recommendations for reducing exposure. The results showed that homes where the recommendations were followed had significant reductions in airborne VOCs and reported improvements in CI symptoms.

Relevance: The findings underscore the importance of consumer education for improving indoor air quality to manage CI symptoms.

Link: Link to study

This collection of studies and sources provides strong scientific backing for the need to clean up both personal environments and the planet. By reducing exposure to environmental toxins and improving air quality, we can significantly lower the risk of various health conditions—from cancer and heart disease to autism, autoimmune diseases, and neurodegenerative disorders. These studies emphasize the importance of taking action at both an individual and societal level to protect our health and the well-being of future generations.

Books for the General Public

Here's a list of some relevant books for the lay public that cover topics like Mast Cell Activation Syndrome (MCAS), chemical exposures, environmental health, and related natural wellness strategies:

"Never Bet Against Occam: Mast Cell Activation Disease and the Modern Epidemics of Chronic Illness and Medical Complexity" by Lawrence B. Afrin, MD

Focuses on MCAS and chronic illnesses linked to mast cell disorders.

"Chemical Exposures: Low Levels and High Stakes" by Nicholas Ashford and Claudia Miller

Discusses the health impacts of low-level chemical exposures and how they can trigger chronic illnesses.

"Human Ecology and Susceptibility to the Chemical Environment" by Theron G. Randolph, MD

A pioneering work on chemical sensitivity and its links to various health conditions.

"Toxic" by Neil Nathan, MD

Explores how mold toxicity, Lyme disease, and chemical sensitivities affect health, and offers treatment options.

"The Allergy Solution: Unlock the Surprising, Hidden Truth about Why You Are Sick and How to Get Well" by Leo Galland, MD

Offers solutions for allergy sufferers, addressing food allergies, environmental triggers, and ways to heal.

"The Mold Survival Guide: For Your Home and for Your Health" by Jeffrey C. May and Connie L. May

Focuses on identifying and mitigating mold-related health problems, which are often linked to chemical sensitivities.

"The Toxin Solution: How Hidden Poisons in the Air, Water, Food, and Products We Use Are Destroying Our Health—and What We Can Do to Fix It" by Joseph Pizzorno, ND

Provides strategies for detoxifying the body and improving health by reducing exposure to environmental toxins.

"Toxic Home/Conscious Home: A Mindful Approach to Wellness at Home" by Rob Brown, MD

Offers guidance on how to reduce exposure to toxins in the home environment and improve wellness.

"The Autoimmune Fix: How to Stop the Hidden Autoimmune Damage That Keeps You Sick, Fat, and Tired Before It Turns Into Disease" by Tom O'Bryan

Covers how environmental factors, including toxins, contribute to autoimmune diseases and offers actionable solutions.

"Clean, Green, and Lean: Get Rid of the Toxins That Make You Fat" by Walter Crinnion, ND

Explores the connection between toxins and weight gain, and offers detox strategies for better health.

"Chemical Sensitivity: The Truth About Environmental Illness" by Sherry A. Rogers, MD

Focuses on chemical sensitivities, how they manifest in different health conditions, and natural solutions for recovery.

"MCS: Multiple Chemical Sensitivities: The Invisible Illness" by Deborah Dadd

A guide for understanding and managing Multiple Chemical Sensitivity, offering practical tips for living with the condition.

"The Healthy Home: Simple Truths to Protect Your Family from Hidden Household Dangers" by Myron Wentz, PhD, and Dave Wentz

Discusses common household toxins and how to reduce exposure for better family health.

"Your Brain on Food: How Chemicals Control Your Thoughts and Feelings" by Gary Wenk, PhD

Explains how environmental chemicals, including food additives and toxins, impact brain health and mood.

"The Detox Prescription: Supercharge Your Health with 60 Recipes and a Three-Day Detox Plan" by Woodson Merrell, MD

Offers a dietary approach to detoxification, emphasizing clean eating and natural methods to eliminate toxins.

"The Allergy and Asthma Cure: A Complete 8-Step Nutritional Program" by Fred Pescatore, MD

Focuses on treating allergies and asthma through natural diet and lifestyle changes, reducing exposure to allergens and toxins.

"How to Grow Fresh Air: 50 Houseplants that Purify Your Home or Office" by B.C. Wolverton

Discusses how houseplants can help reduce indoor air pollutants and improve health.

"Toxic-Free: How to Protect Your Health and Home from the Chemicals That Are Making You Sick" by Debra Lynn Dadd

A practical guide to reducing toxic chemical exposure in your home and improving overall health.

"Non-Toxic: Guide to Living Healthy in a Chemical World" by Aly Cohen, MD

Provides comprehensive information on reducing exposure to environmental toxins and adopting a non-toxic lifestyle.

"The Whole-Body Guide to Gut Health: Heal Your Gut Through Diet, Exercise, and Stress Reduction" by Dr. Ellen Vora

Discusses how gut health is impacted by toxins and stress, and offers natural strategies to heal the digestive system.

These books cover a wide range of relevant topics, from understanding chemical sensitivities and their health impacts to practical guides on detoxifying your home and improving overall wellness through environmental changes. ***For even more tips, ideas, and resources, visit DrIrisBell.com***